HE OBEYED GOD

HE OBEYED GOD

THE STORY OF

Albert Benjamin Simpson

BY PAT DYS
AND LINDA CORBIN

CHRISTIAN PUBLICATIONS

Camp Hill, Pennsylvania

Christian Publications
*Publishing House of The Christian
and Missionary Alliance*
3825 Hartzdale Drive, Camp Hill, PA 17011

The mark of *vibrant faith*

Library of Congress Catalog Card No: 86-71048
© 1986 by Christian Publications. All rights reserved
ISBN: 0-87509-382-5
Printed in the United States of America

#20691110

CONTENTS

CHAPTER

1

He Obeys His Parents

THE SUN WAS SETTING, and he knew he should go home, but Josh didn't want to. He liked the little island where he was sitting, liked it especially at sunset.

Josh liked the way the colors changed. The leaves of the trees turned from green to black as the sunlight behind them displayed its prism of colors. He liked the way the breezes moved from daytime brisk to evening gentle.

Josh liked to watch as the water calmed just in time to reflect a mirror image of the two arched foot bridges that stretched off either side of the island. He also liked to watch Noah D. Webster, the island's only resident, waddle to its favorite spot beside the water and settle down for the night.

Although the island was in the center of a pond in the center of a village, Josh felt he was far from everything when he was in this spot. He liked that. It gave him a chance to figure things out. He had many things to figure out these days.

Someimes he just tried to figure out things about the world in general, starting with the island he was on. It was a very small island, just right for one small boy, a duck and "Sir," the elderly man who frequently shared its solitude.

Surrounding Josh's island was The Village, of an island, too, where hundreds of older people lived, retired from the larger world of North America, which was an island, too. From school, Josh knew North America was an island. He wondered how many of these islands were connected to each other by bridges, like his island was to The Village and The Village to North America. *Airplanes are sort of bridges to the islands of the sea,* he thought to himself, remembering his trips across the oceans from where he had been born.

Josh had lived most of his life on a medium-sized island half way around the world from where he now sat. That was where his parents had been missionaries. In fact, that was where he had been born—a blond-haired American boy in a world where all the other children were dark-haired. Sometimes he wondered why he couldn't have just stayed on that other

island with his dark-haired friends. Why had
he had to cross the first bridge out of that island?

Leaving that other island had changed his
life very much. Since then he had crossed
bridge after bridge until he found himself on
this island with Noah. The chain of events was
hard for him to understand. Angrily he kicked
a stone in front of him, causing Noah the duck
to flutter from its nighttime nest.

"Whoa, Josh," a familiar voice spoke out of
the shadowing laurel tree branches. "I thought
you and Noah were friends!" Josh grinned at
the sight of his friend, "Sir." Samuel T. Surr was
99 years old. The good care and pleasant sur-
roundings of his retirement home had restored
his weary body. His mind had always been
vigorous, and he kept it so even now.

Josh and "Sir" had met on this very island
almost a year ago, and they had become
friends immediately. Josh called the old man
"Sir" because of that first meeting. Josh had
asked, "And what is your name, sir?" The man
replied with a chuckle that had been practiced
nearly a century, "That's it, boy! My name is
Surr—Samuel T. Surr." So ever after, Josh
called the old man "Sir."

Josh made room for Samuel Surr to sit down

beside him on the bench. Together they watched the duck return to its nest.

"I do like Noah D. Webster," Josh said after a few moments.

"That's good," replied Samuel. "By the way, why is his middle initial 'D'?" The conversation was as aimless as the watery, circular ripples that Noah had left behind in the pond.

"It stands for *Duck*. I didn't want him to be mistaken for the man who wrote the dictionary," Josh answered.

Samuel's chuckle was friendly, and Joshua settled against the old man's shoulder. The two were silent for a long while.

At last Samuel asked, "What were the thoughts that were flying on that stone you kicked?"

Josh understood the question to mean that Samuel was ready to listen to him. "Sir, why are my parents missionaries?"

It was a big question, and Samuel approached it slowly. "Because they obeyed God," he answered.

"You're not a missionary, Sir. Did you ·disobey God?"

"Obeying God," the old man replied, "is strange and wonderful. It requires many things of us. First, we need to know God so we will recognize who we are to obey. Then we need to listen long and carefully to what He is saying to us. When we finally get a picture of what God wants us to be, we need to be willing to jump into the picture and take our place in it without arguing or holding back. That is obeying God."

Silence. "Oh," Josh commented.

"I guess that didn't make much sense, did it?" Samuel continued. "Would you like me to tell you a story about a man I once met who knew God and saw God's picture for his life and willingly became part of it? That man knew what it was to obey God."

"I love your stories, Sir," Josh responded, settling comfortably within the old man's circling arm, rhythmically swinging his feet below the bench.

"I met this man in New York City when I was a young newspaper reporter there," Samuel began. "I happened to come upon him in a crowded, poor section of the city. I was attracted by the sight of this tall, impressive man helping a sad, broken-down young man. My older partner recognized him as the out-of-the-ordinary minister whose preaching and work for the Lord had been headline news for years."

"What was his name?" Josh inquired.

"A.B. Simpson was his name." Samuel answered slowly, speaking the words with a faraway look in his eyes, as if he had momentarily forgotten Josh at his side.

"Did the *A.B.* stand for alphabet like *D.* stands for duck?" Josh teased.

The old man snapped back to the present. "It stood for Albert Benjamin," he said, tweaking Josh's nose playfully.

"Albert Benjamin Simpson was born in 1843—almost 150 years ago. And, like you, Josh, he was born on an island. He was born on Prince Edward Island in Canada."

"I like islands," Josh commented, warming at once to the story.

"Prince Edward Island is one of the world's loveliest islands. Albert's family had lived there many years before he was born. His grandparents had arrived there from Scotland in 1775—part of a group of pilgrims who left the Old World for the New so they could worship God as they believed they should. They were determined to obey God, even if it meant a dangerous, difficult trip to a new land.

"Albert's parents also wanted to obey God. And from the earliest days of Albert's life they taught him how to obey. They set a good example for him to follow. Albert could not help but notice that they worked hard with their hands to provide for their nine children. He noticed that his father could turn a small farm and mill into a good business by using his muscles and strong will. But he also saw how gentle and loving his father was toward the family. His words were kind. He controlled his temper.

"Albert's mother also taught her children obedience by her example. Her life was not easy. One of Albert's older brothers died as a small boy. The family moved to Chatham, Ontario. There a fierce epidemic swept through the town and one of Albert's sisters died. The family feared the sickness and moved again. This time they settled on an isolated farm several miles from the town. Times were hard, and the family was lonely—especially Albert's mother, who missed her friends.

"Sometimes at night Albert could hear his mother crying softly. He would not have known what to do about it except that his mother had taught him to pray. His mother talked to God about everything. So Albert prayed, asking God to comfort his mother. From then on, Albert always talked everything over with God.

"The example Albert's parents set of diligent work, kindness, gentleness, self-control, prayer, love and faith were his earliest lessons in obeying God. Those things became part of Albert's life, too, just as they must become part of all our lives, Josh, if we want to truly please God.

"But Albert's parents taught him obedience in other ways, also. The family had rules, and every member had to keep the rules or face stern punishment. One family rule was that Sunday was only for worshiping God. Albert knew the rule, yet occasionally he wandered outside on Sundays to play rather than to stay in the house reading his Bible and praying.

"The punishment for such disobedience was a whipping. Albert dreaded those whippings. His older brother told him to pretend to be very sorry for what he had done. And it was a good idea to be reading his Bible when his father came to punish.

"Stop snickering, Josh," Samuel scolded, interrupting the story. "It was wrong for Albert to only pretend he was sorry he had disobeyed. And I don't believe he often used that means to escape punishment.

"For the most part, Albert began early obeying his parents and God. He knew it was the best way to live. He and the family attended church faithfully—a Presbyterian church nine miles from their home. After church, it was catechism time. Albert and his brothers and sisters were drilled in the 150 questions in the Shorter Catechism that explained important truths of the Bible. To memorize all the questions and answers and to listen to long explanations was hard. But obedience was expected, and Albert learned what was required, even when it was not easy or very interesting."

The old man shifted his position as he realized how late it was getting. "My young friend," he said, "you had better get on home before dark if you are going to obey your dad and mom!"

"But, Sir, you haven't finished the story, have you?" Josh sounded disappointed.

"There's much more to it," Samuel replied. "I'll have to tell you the rest another time. Shall we plan to meet here again tomorrow, Josh?"

Josh beamed. "I'll be here!"

"I know you will." The old man squeezed Josh's shoulder, then rose from the bench where the two had been seated. The colors had long since disappeared from the quiet pond. Josh watched Samuel pick up his hat from the post of the bench where he had

CHAPTER
2

He Meets His Savior

NEXT MORNING, JOSH was the first to arrive on the island. He was intently watching Noah D. Webster when Samuel Surr arrived.

"Do you think Noah acts sort of different lately?" Josh asked, without even saying hello.

"How different can a duck act?" replied the old man. "Maybe she doesn't like us watching her build her nest."

"*She!*" Josh whirled around in surprise. "Is Noah a *she?*"

"I guess it's the she duck that build nests," Samuel commented.

"Oh, no!" moaned Josh. "What a name for a mother duck!"

"I don't suppose she minds," said Samuel as they turned toward the bench. The two sat silently for some time, just enjoying being together as two very good friends will do.

Josh broke the silence, small boys being less able to remain quiet than old men. "Tell me the rest of the story of your friend, A.B.C. Simpson, Sir," he begged.

"Just *A.B.* Simpson, Josh," Samuel corrected. He chuckled to let Josh know he recognized his joke and appreciated it. "But he wasn't really my friend. I'm not that old to have known him long. But I did admire what I knew of him. Let's see—where was I in the story? I forget sometimes. I *am* old enough to be forgetful."

"You never forget anything," Josh reassured his friend. "You were telling me how Albert as a young boy learned to be obedient."

"Oh, yes. I was telling you about his early lessons from his parents. Did I tell you how he put some of those lessons into practice?"

"Tell me!" coaxed Josh.

"Well, part of obeying God is believing God. And early in his life Albert learned to believe God. First, he learned to believe that God can be trusted. He had already seen how God cared for them through the long move to Chatham and in sickness. But several frightening accidents clearly showed Albert that God was in control of his life and could be trusted.

"Once Albert was climbing the scaffolding of a building under construction when a loose board tipped and he fell. Flailing his arms, he barely caught hold of a piece of wood as he dropped toward the ground far below. He screamed for help. Just when he thought he could hold on no longer, help came, and his life was spared.

"Twice accidents with a horse knocked Albert unconscious. Once he almost drowned when he went into water over his head. As the water closed in over him, it seemed in a flash he saw his whole life as it might have been. He even imagined, Josh, a newspaper story such as I might have written, reporting his death to his grieving family. Coming close to death like that makes us think seriously about God and what He wants of us."

Samuel paused to glance at Josh, wondering if the story might be too frightening. But Josh was merely serious, as he often was, waiting patiently for the story to continue.

"Josh, after his accidents, Albert suddenly had a great desire to know God. He had seen that God could be trusted to spare his life. Coming close to death, he thought about heaven and felt certain that if he had died, he would not have gone there."

"You mean your friend was not a Christian?" Josh asked with surprise. "I know if I die I'll go to heaven."

Samuel's faded blue eyes, always so twinkling and happy, softened to seriousness as he looked at Josh. "My little friend," he said, "that is the most important matter in your life. I'm glad it is settled. It is for me, too. But, yes, Albert at that early age was not a Christian, for he had never really understood how to believe God for his salvation from sin. That understanding came some time later, although while he was still young."

"How did Albert find the way to be saved?" Josh wondered aloud.

"It was while he was going to school. Albert was a good student. He studied so hard that, while his mind grew in knowledge, his body became weak and sick. He became so weak, in fact, that he thought he might die.

"In his weakness, Albert sensed a great and dreadful fear coming over him. He begged his father to pray for him. His father prayed. Still the fear was there. He thought of his sinfulness. He knew from his study of the Shorter Catechism that God punishes sinners. What he had never understood was that God also *loves* sinners. He loves them so much that He sent His Son, Jesus, to die for them.

"Albert prayed that God would not let him die until he was a forgiven sinner. Once he was so frightened and ill that he prayed all day for his salvation. He asked his friends to pray for him that day, too. By night he still was not at peace with God. But he was sure of two things: one, God *was able* to save him and, two, God would not let him die until he was saved.

"Time passed. Health returned slowly. One day, Albert was strong enough to visit in the home of a minister friend. In the minister's library, Albert found an old, musty book. The book was unappealing in appearance, but in it were just the words he needed. They seemed to jump out at him. He could never forget them.

> *The first good work you will ever do is to believe on the Lord Jesus Christ. Until you do this, all your works, prayers and tears are useless. Believing on the Lord Jesus is to believe that He saves you according to His Word. He receives and saves you here and now, for He has said, "Him that cometh to me I will in no wise cast out."*

"Albert fell on his knees. Looking up to heaven, he prayed, 'Lord Jesus, You have said, "Him that cometh to me I will in no wise cast out." You know how long and how earnestly I have tried to come, but I did not know how. Now I come the best way that I know. I believe that You receive me and save me and that I am Your child because I have believed Your Word. Father, You are mine and I am Yours.'

"The battle was over. Albert knew he had been forgiven. He knew he was now a believer. The God he had been taught to obey he now could obey with a willing heart, for he loved God with a deep love. The joy of knowing and loving God was his strength for the rest of his life."

"That almost makes me cry," said Josh softly.

Samuel's voice, usually strong, quavered a bit. "Yes, Josh, God's love for us makes me cry sometimes. But I cry for joy. I am thankful that *you* have put *your* trust in Jesus Christ, Josh. You are very precious to me. Nothing makes me happier than knowing you are obeying God.

"You asked me yesterday why your parents had decided to be missionaries, and I told you it was because they had obeyed God. Believing God for salvation is the first step in obedience. But obedience to God continues. Watch your Dad and Mom carefully as they seek God's way for their lives, and you will learn much about obedience."

Josh thought about Sir's advice. "Is that the end of the story?"

"No, but do you hear those chimes from the church?"

"Oh!" Josh exclaimed, springing to his feet. "It's lunch time and I'm late!" With a quick motion, he tossed the feather he had been toying with into the pond. He was tempted to follow it with a stone, but he didn't delay.

"See you later, Sir!" Josh said as he turned to race home.

CHAPTER
3

He Gives Himself to God

TIME PASSED PLEASANTLY at The Village where Samuel lived and in the nearby, quiet neighborhood where Joshua lived. The ever-present sunshine lifted people's spirits. The warmth made outdoor living easy. There were plenty of interesting things to do, even for Josh, whose delicate health kept him from doing what most boys his age did.

Samuel T. Surr's steady presence more than made up for what Josh missed in friendships his own age. The two spent time together often. Samuel had a century of stories to tell. He told them well, and Josh was a ready listener. Josh, in turn, had remarkable stories of his own to tell—more than most seven-year-olds. With Samuel's example, he was becoming a good storyteller, too.

Joshua had just finished telling an especially funny adventure about a midnight prank at boarding school when he became suddenly serious. It was so sudden that Samuel's chuckle was left suspended in midair.

"What is it, Josh?" Samuel asked.

"I just remembered how sick I was the next day," replied Josh.

"That should have taught you to behave!" Samuel teased.

"I don't think missing one night of sleep made me sick, Sir," Josh replied accurately with a smile. Then he was serious again. "But from then on I have never been well. Sir, my getting sick has made so many problems. My parents are not as happy as they used to be, and I don't think they are just worried about me. Do you think they are sorry that they had to stop being missionaries? Remember, Sir, you said they became missionaries because they obeyed God. Are they disobeying Him now? Is that what makes them sad?"

Josh and Samuel were walking along the water's edge, and the wind was strong. Josh's blond hair blew in feathery wisps around his face as he looked up at his elderly friend. Samuel stopped and tamed the wild locks in both his hands. With his hands still on Josh's head, he said, "Those are awfully big thoughts for this little head. But your questions are good ones to talk about."

They continued to walk. "You remember I was telling you about the remarkable preacher from Canada?" Samuel asked.

"I remember."

"You remember that the changes God brought into his boyhood life caused some pain, too. Remember how he heard his mother crying at night? Some changes bring pain, and some pain brings changes. All of it teaches us to obey God and to look for His will in our lives."

They walked, Josh measuring his step to the old man's pace.

"God's ways are not always our ways, but they are always the best. It took Albert Simpson some years to realize this. Hidden back in his babyhood years was a fact that shaped his life, but he was not aware of it for many years. "When Albert was less than two weeks old, his parents took him to their Presbyterian church and offered him to the Lord. Dr. John Geddie, a visiting missionary to the South Seas, prayed for him that God would call him to be a missionary. God honored the obedience of Albert's parents in dedicating their child to Him. In later years, God would claim this life for missionary service, but not in the way his parents perhaps expected. Nor in the way Albert expected, either.

"In fact, Albert wasn't sure what he expected out of life. His parents' godly ambition for their children must have made a deep impression on Albert, for as a young boy he wondered if he would be a minister. To be a minister was good, although he did wish he could do something in life that would be fun.

"He loved adventure. He wished, for example, that his mother wasn't so afraid of guns ever since his uncle had been killed accidentally by one. He would love to be an expert marksman.

"He treasured that idea for a long time. Finally, at age 14, he bought a gun with money he had been able to save. He hid the gun from his parents, occasionally sneaking out to the woods to practice shooting."

"Would my mom be angry!" whistled Joshua.

"Albert's mom was angry, too. She made him return the gun to the shop where he had bought it. Albert did not even get his money back. It was not very willing obedience, but Albert obeyed and then decided that, since life was not much fun anyway, he might as well go ahead and be a minister. Poor Albert! Such a wrong reason to do something so right!"

"Was he ever happy being a minister?" Joshua wanted to know.

"He was. But God had to teach him many things first. Right after Albert decided to be a minister, problems arose. Albert's parents decided Albert's older brother, Howard, should study for the ministry. The family had only enough money to send one son to school. Albert would have to stay home and work on the farm.

"It was a hard blow for young Albert. The boy ventured to stammer, 'Uh, Father, I, uh, would also like to go to school. I am willing to work for my own money if you will just give your permission. I, too, want to be a minister.'

"Albert's father must have remembered the time, years before, when he had dedicated his son to the Lord. He could not say no to such a plea. 'God bless you, my boy.' It was all the encouragement Albert needed. He would begin the long, hard struggle to become a minister, depending daily on God to supply his need.

"Already Albert had learned the basics— reading, writing, arithmetic—at a common school."

"A *what* school?" Josh interrupted.

"A common school—like your elementary school." Samuel continued: "To prepare for high school, Albert and his brother were taught Latin, Greek and higher math by their pastor and another minister."

"Whew!" exclaimed Joshua. "What hard subjects!"

"True. But they were able to learn and to enter Chatham High School. The learning continued, and Albert studied so hard that he became sick. It was while he was recovering that he put his faith in Jesus to save him. You remember my telling you about that. So even in that year of sickness and weakness, God was helping Albert to learn His will."

Josh nodded approval.

"By the time he was 16, with returning health, Albert learned some new lessons in God's school. This very young man, too young to even grow whiskers, became the teacher of a class of 40 people, including some adults! His teaching earned money he needed for college. In every spare moment, he studied for his college entrance exam."

"Was he ever sad about his hard life?" Josh wanted to know.

"No doubt he was. But do you know what kept him moving forward?"

"He grew some whiskers?" Josh's eyes twinkled.

"Josh! Be serious!"

"Well, what then?"

"He was careful not to get away from God. Albert had read about great Christians who made a written agreement with God. He decided to write one, too. First, he spent a whole day praying. He did not even eat. Then he wrote a long agreement. He gave himself completely to God. He claimed from God all that God offered. He signed his name to the paper. Never did he throw that paper away. Two times later in his life when he was not as close to God as he wanted to be, he reread the agreement and renewed it.

"You see, Josh, though it was not always easy to obey God, Albert very wisely gave himself to God and asked God to show him His will and how he should live."

The two had walked all the way around The Village. Now they stood at the bridge between The Village and Joshua's neighborhood. "Josh," said Samuel, "much later in his life, Albert Simpson wrote that he never stopped thanking God for the hard decisions. I hope you, too, can thank God for the hard things your family is facing. Hard things teach us to obey God as we trust Him to show us His way."

"I'll try," Josh promised.

The small boy with big thoughts crossed over the bridge.

CHAPTER

4

He Becomes a Minister

SIR! COME QUICK!" JOSH said as he noticed Samuel Surr approaching the bridge to their favorite small island. "Noah has 11 eggs in her nest!"

Josh took Samuel's hand and tried to hurry the old man, at the same time being mindful of his aged step.

"Well, look at that!" Samuel said as they neared the heap of broken, dead reeds on which lay the clear, clay-colored eggs dotted with dark brown. "I wonder—"

A series of short, rough croaks and cackles stopped the two and made them step back.

O-o-o-o, I guess she doesn't like us so close," said Josh.

"Just obeying the instincts God placed in her to protect her family," observed Samuel as he rested himself on the bench. "How is *your* family, Josh? Are your Dad and Mom happier than when last we met?"

"We're thanking the Lord for problems!"

Josh's tone was both serious and playful. Samuel wasn't sure he understood, but he didn't pursue the question. He was at least glad that his advice had been heeded.

"I didn't finish telling you about A.B. Simpson's problems, did I?" Samuel asked. Josh prepared to listen to the ongoing story, shading himself from the sun with Samuel's cap.

"He sure had a hard time of it getting to be a preacher!" said Josh.

"Oh, preaching seemed to come almost naturally to him," answered Samuel. "Why, he was only about 10 when he preached his first sermon."

Josh could not quite tell if Samuel was serious. "Ten?" he asked incredulously.

"That's right. It was on a Sunday when the Simpson children had not gone with their parents to church. So the huge farmhouse kitchen became their church, and Albert preached his sermon to his brothers and sisters.

"But when did he become a *real* preacher?" Josh wanted to know.

"Well, before he could even go to college, he had to be tested by a group of ministers. They questioned him to see what sort of a young man he was. Would he make a good minister? Had he let Jesus into his heart? Was he walking close to God? Did he understand the Bible? Had God really called him to the ministry?

"He even had to read them a sermon he had written. Face to face with those men and their searching questions, Albert must have been thankful all over again for the lessons he had learned on knowing God and His will."

"And he must have been glad for the practice he got when he preached to his brothers and sisters!" said Joshua.

"I suppose so," chuckled Samuel. "And he did pass the exam so that he could enroll in Knox College in Toronto."

"Good!" Joshua exclaimed with relief. "At last his troubles were over."

"You've never been to college if you think that!" Samuel chuckled again before turning serious. "College brought Albert some of his greatest struggles."

"More hard studies?" ventured Josh.

"Yes, that was true, but you remember he was a good student. His big struggle came when he forgot to guard his walk with God. His roommate, an older student than he, had wild parties several times a week in their room. He knew the parties were wrong. And as he sat and watched week after week, he noticed that his love for God was going away.

He didn't enjoy reading his Bible or praying anymore. God seemed far away and Albert missed His closeness.

"But Albert had not forgotten what he had learned about obedience to God. Again, he took the covenant he had signed before God and promised God to be obedient. God helped him to resist the temptation to join in the parties.

"But other problems arose. He was sure that it was God's will for him to be at Knox College, but how could he pay his bills without even a penny? More than once he went outside at night and threw himself down on the grass. There in the darkness and, as he put it, in the 'deeper darkness of soul,' he prayed to God for the money he needed. And God did not fail him. He received some scholarships—money given to good students so they can continue to study—and he also won a writing contest.

"Through it all, Albert learned an important lesson. God expects us to believe Him. We must believe God if we expect Him to answer our prayers. Josh, remember that important truth. Before God answers our prayer, we must obey Him by believing what He says."

Josh pushed Samuel's cap back on his head

and looked up at his friend. "Didn't anything good happen to Albert in college?"

"Good things? Of course! The struggles were good things. They helped to teach—"

"Yes, I know," Josh interrupted. "But did any *happy* things happen to Albert?"

"Albert fell in love with a young woman by the name of Margaret Henry. He married her just after graduation."

"Oh," exclaimed Josh in mock disgust. "I said *happy* things." They laughed together.

"Well," Samuel tried again, "there was his first Christmas vacation."

"Now *that's* happy!" Josh exclaimed. He remembered returning home at Christmastime from boarding school when his parents were missionaries.

"Yes, but for Albert, going home was mixed with fear. He had been asked to preach at a church near his home. In the audience would be all his family as well as friends and neighbors. He carefully prepared his sermon. Then he went out into the woods with the squirrels and the trees and practiced what he would say. Even so, he did not dare look at his family and friends when he preached.

"But God saw him through that sermon and hundreds more in the 48 years that he preached. Albert Simpson's messages became a great delight to all who heard him. But never did he forget to give God the glory for his skill."

Samuel had come to a break in his story. He changed his position on the bench before continuing. "Albert not only graduated from college, but he also graduated from the seminary—the school where ministers get special training for their future work. Then he had to appear before the same group of ministers who had talked to him before he entered Knox College. He passed their examination and was then ready to become a minister himself.

"Two churches asked Albert Simpson to be their pastor. He chose Knox Presbyterian Church in Hamilton, Ontario, the one he thought would be the hardest job. He wanted to be forced to work hard and to become a fine minister.

"It seemed as though this was exactly the church for which God had been preparing him. After all his years of learning how to know God and His will and learning how to obey God, Albert Benjamin Simpson had found his place. The people of the church loved their minister, and he loved them. During nine years in Hamilton, the church added

750 new members, paid off their debts and gave generously to foreign missions.

"Even my friends in the newspaper business took notice of this young minister. Often the newspapers printed his sermons for the whole community to read," said Samuel, remembering his days as a reporter.

"Wouldn't you think that would make him happy for the rest of his life?" Samuel asked. "And, besides, four of the six children he and his wife had were born while they were in Hamilton. Yes, those were happy days for the Simpsons.

"But then, as in your family, Josh, while they were obeying God and seeing His blessing on their lives, there came a change."

"What was that?" Josh wanted to know.

"I'll tell you another time," promised Samuel.

"Now?" teased Josh.

The old man slowly rose to his feet, at the same time retrieving his cap from Josh. "Next time!"

CHAPTER
5

He Discovers God's Will

JOSH AND SAMUEL HAD been almost daily companions for a long time. Josh felt at peace in the company of the loving old man. Although he did not realize it, he was learning much from the stories his aged friend told.

Then, just as Noah D. Webster's clay-colored eggs were about to hatch, Josh had to go on a long trip to see another doctor about his sickness. He and his parents had to be gone several days. Josh knew Samuel would be keeping close watch on Noah so that he could report progress. Still, Josh was very happy to get back home.

He headed immediately for the island. Sure enough, there was Samuel, intently watching Noah's nest from a safe distance. The old man did not hear Josh approaching. Josh touched Samuel's arm, and Samuel turned, startled.

"Josh! You're back!" he exclaimed with deep satisfaction in his voice. He gave Josh a hug. "I'm happy to see you again! Look what is happening in Noah D. Webster's nest." Samuel turned the boy toward the nest, pulling aside a branch so he could see.

Josh whistled ever so softly, for he did not want to frighten mama duck. "Mrs. Noah D. Webster, your family is arriving!" he whispered.

They turned away, not wishing to disturb the nest. "You know, Josh," Samuel began, "I've been doing some study, and I think that *D.* in her name needs to be changed. I don't think she's a duck."

Josh was puzzled. "She looks like a duck."

"Yes, but see her slate gray color and her white bill? And watch her swim." They watched as Mrs. Webster swam buoyantly, nodding her head as she paddled. Then with an upward jump she submerged in search of food. "Those," Samuel continued, "are the motions of a bird often mistaken for a duck—a coot, spelled c-o-o-t."

Josh never questioned Samuel's vast store of knowledge. "Okay, her name is Mrs. Noah *C.* Webster. I hope she doesn't . . ." His sentence trailed off as the bird, heavy in flight, ran across the surface of the pond to reach take-off speed.

"I wonder what she's up to now," Josh said.

"Wild creatures generally do what they are supposed to do in God's order for them," remarked Samuel.

"How do *we* know what God wants *us* to do?" Josh asked. Josh's quickness in applying Samuel's statement about wild creatures led the old man to suspect that Josh had faced some decisions during their days apart. He knew Josh would tell him when he was ready, so he didn't press him. Rather, he answered his question.

"Some things God wants us to do are easy enough to discover. We can read them right in the Bible. At other times, we are truly puzzled to know what we should do. At times like that, I believe we must start doing the simplest thing at hand. While we are obeying God in that small matter, He will show us what to do next."

"Hm-m-m," Josh said thoughtfully.

"Albert B. Simpson faced that same question."

"The last time you told me about him, Mr. Simpson was facing a big change in his life," Josh said, adding, "like the one our family is facing."

"The big change came when Mr. Simpson moved his family out of their happy home in

Hamilton, Ontario, to Louisville, Kentucky. Mr. Simpson had been invited to be minister of Chestnut Street Presbyterian Church in Louisville. The Civil War in the United States was just over, and the churches in Louisville were still divided over the question of slavery. There was much hatred among the churches.

"Where should Mr. Simpson start? What should he do? He knew before any work for the Lord could be done in that city, there must come a change in the hearts of many people. He decided he should start with his fellow ministers. So he invited them to meet for prayer. As the ministers got their hearts right with God, it happened. The old hatreds of the Civil War were forgiven. Pastors who had seldom spoken to each other shook hands and became friends again.

"It was a start. But why not continue it? The ministers planned a citywide evangelistic campaign. Thousands came out each evening to the large Library Hall to hear the evangelist and the musicians. Hundreds of these people found their lives changed by God.

"When the campaign ended, Mr. Simpson wanted to continue to reach out to the city of Louisville. So his church rented Library Hall each Sunday evening, and there Mr. Simpson continued preaching the gospel to the thousands of people who packed the Hall. Louisville became a different city. The newspapers noticed the difference and reported the services each week. I wish I could have been there," Samuel added wistfully, thinking of his former career as a newspaper reporter.

"Soon news reached the papers that Chestnut Street Presbyterian Church was going to build a large new auditorium in which to hold the weekly services. Mr. Simpson cautioned his church against making it a costly building that would prevent them from giving money to missions. He knew that expensive buildings could sometimes make a church selfish.

"You'll remember, Josh, that Mr. Simspon had learned to know God well. He had been careful to find out God's will for his life. He knew God wanted him to reach people with the message of how to know God and have their sins forgiven. That purpose stayed uppermost in his mind whatever he did.

"Once, late at night, Mr. Simpson thought of a man in the city who needed to be saved. It was a stormy night outside, and Mr. Simpson wished the thought would go away. But it didn't. At last, Mr. Simpson went to the man's house and knocked on the door. The man was surprised to see the great preacher, dripping wet from the rain. Mr. Simpson explained that he had come because he was anxious for the man to be saved. That very night the man turned his heart over to Jesus.

"Another time, Mr. Simpson came across a young girl. He tried to explain the love of God to her. But she was so neglected and poor that she could not begin to understand. Mr. Simpson asked his church people to leave their fine homes and visit this poor girl with gifts of food. As she began to understand human love, she was able to understand God's love. In turn, she was able to love God for sending His Son to be her Savior.

"While helping people, Mr. Simpson was careful to guard his own walk with God. In that, too, he found that God wants us to do first what is at hand. Mr. Simpson longed to be closer to God, but he didn't know how to get there. He shut himself away from his family, his congregation and his community so that he could seek God. He stopped visiting the sick, the lonely, the needy. But he felt no nearer to God.

"Crying out to God for help, Mr. Simpson felt he should look into his Bible. There he read, '[Jesus] is not here; he is risen. He goes before you...." Suddenly Mr. Simpson realized that he would not get closer to God by shutting himself out from the rest of the world. God was out there where people were in great need, and Mr. Simpson had been neglecting them.

"Mr. Simpson hurried out to visit those needy people. As he began to pray with them, he suddenly felt God very close to him. This was exactly what he had been wishing for. Only as he obeyed God did he find God near to him. And in his own joy he was able to make others happy.

"So you see, Josh, as we obey God in the things we already know we must do, God will show us what else to do. He will draw us close to Himself and make us a blessing to others."

The pair was silent as Samuel concluded his story. Josh picked up a slender leaf, carefully tearing it into tiny threads as he thought through what Samuel had just said.

Suddenly, Josh sprang from the park bench. "I have to tell them!" he announced. And he darted off the island.

He Gets a Healthy Body

WHEN JOSH RETURNED to the island, he found Samuel seated on the bench just as he had left him the day before. It was almost as though he had never moved. Only now Samuel was singing. Josh stopped just out of view to listen:

I will say yes to Jesus,
To all that He commands,
I will hasten to do His bidding
With willing heart and hands;
I will listen to hear His whispers,
And learn His will each day,
And always gladly answer yes
Whatever He may say.

I will say yes to Jesus,
Yes, Lord forever . . .

"Oh, Josh, I drowned out your footsteps with my singing!" exclaimed Samuel as at last he

49

spied his young friend. "You are here early to-day."

Samuel motioned for Josh to take his usual place beside him. Josh sat down, but only on the edge of the bench, half facing the old man.

"I had to tell you," Josh began. "You know how confused my parents have been, wanting to go back to being missionaries but also wanting me to get well."

"I know it has been quite a struggle," Samuel replied sympathetically.

"Well, it's decided," Josh continued. "We're going to stay here until I get well. When I told them the last part of Mr. Simpson's story, they suddenly looked at each other like they had discovered something. They said, 'We know what is at hand to do first. Let's do it and see where God leads us from there.'" Josh was beaming as he related the incident.

"Our family is happy again! Isn't that exciting, Sir? Isn't it?" Josh had expected to find more enthusiasm on Samuel's face.

"I was just thinking, Josh," Samuel said. "There is something you can do also in this situation."

"Me?" Josh asked.

"Your sickness has been at the center of your family's problem. Have you thought of asking God to make you well? Mr. Simpson, you remember, learned early that if you expect God to meet a need in your life, you must trust Him. There came a time when he realized this was true for his health needs as well.

"Remember how sick Mr. Simpson became from studying too hard? Throughout the years in Hamilton and Louisville, he often needed to rest and guard his strength.

"He had a weak heart. He feared even climbing a small hill or a flight of steps would be too much for him. Later, when he became sick again, he went to rest at a campground in Old Orchard Beach, in Maine. There he carefully studied what God's Word has to say about God's willingness to heal our bodies. He listened at the camp to Bible teachers who urged people to trust God to heal their sicknesses.

"Mr. Simpson left the campground to walk down by the ocean. There is a rock there known as Gugen's Rock. As Mr. Simpson sat there watching the waves, he noticed a small piece of seaweed wash up onto the shore. It was left there for a few moments, and then another wave washed in and swept it back out to sea. The next wave carried it up on the beach again, and the following wave washed it back out to sea.

"Mr. Simpson was fascinated. 'Little sea-weed,' he said, 'I'm going to put you where no cruel wave will ever touch you again!' So saying, he got up and gently carried the seaweed to high, dry ground. Suddenly, Mr. Simpson saw a lesson in that piece of seaweed. *He* was like the little seaweed, swept back and forth by unbelief or pride. And all the while God was able and willing to deliver him.

"Leaving the seaside, Mr. Simpson found a secluded spot in the pine woods where he could be alone with God. There he promised God three things. First, he would believe what God's Word said about His being able to heal sick bodies. Never again would he question what the Bible said. Second, he would believe that God was making him well, and he would never doubt that, either. Third, he would use his new health for God's glory and the good of other people."

"Did God make him well?" Josh interrupted.

"You tell me. The very next day, some of his friends wanted him to go mountain climbing with them. The mountain was 3,000 feet high. Always before, even small hills had left him breathless. But he thought that if he feared to go, it would be because he did not believe that

God had made him well. So he decided to go—
but he would go in God's strength only.

"At first, the climb was very difficult. But as
Mr. Simpson reached out to God by faith, he
received God's strength. He got to the top of
the mountain, and it seemed to him like the
gates of heaven. He had trusted God, and God
had been faithful to him. For the rest of his life
he trusted in God for the health and strength
that he needed.

"After God became his strength, Mr. Simpson could work harder than ever before. He
said four times harder! Besides being a minister, holding three services every Sunday and
two each weekday, he published a weekly missions magazine and a number of books.

"After Mr. and Mrs. Simpson had seen Jesus
heal their daughter of a serious fever, they
opened their own home so that sick people
could learn about Jesus, the Healer, and be
prayed for. Later, when their home was not
large enough for everyone who wanted to
come, the church provided a special house
where sick people could go and hear about Jesus and His power to heal.

"Mr. Simpson became very famous because
of the people who were healed in their bodies
through his teaching. But always, he pointed

people to Jesus. For Mr. Simpson, knowing God and being obedient to Him was even more important than being well. He preached all the good news about Jesus and urged people to believe on Him as their Savior and the One who could make them obedient to God. Then, when they were living their lives according to God's design, and only then, could they trust God to make them well in body."

Samuel turned on the bench so that he could face his young friend. "Josh," he said, "I'm thinking that you are at that point. You told me that Jesus is your Savior, and I see that you are very open to God's will and obedient to what He teaches you. Do you think you could trust God also to make you well?"

Joshua did not hesitate. "I could—I *will*, Sir! Wait till I tell my parents!"

Samuel reached out a hand to detain Josh. "No, Josh, don't tell them yet. My advice is that you first tell God. Then, without saying anything to anyone, see what God will do. You are old enough to ask for what God has promised."

"I am?"

"Yes, you are," Samuel replied. "Jesus never refused the little ones while He was on earth. He won't refuse you, either. Trust Him!"

The two parted quietly. Josh was thinking

carefully about what he should do. And Samuel was deep in conversation with his Lord. He prayed that Josh's faith would be honored. He prayed that God who had saved Josh from his sins and made him His own would get all the glory.

The setting sun flashed a momentary blaze of color before it disappeared. It was almost as if God was giving His blessing to the faith of Josh and Samuel.

CHAPTER
7

He Hears God's "Go Tell"

YOUNG JOSH'S FAITH had grown quickly in the past few weeks, as had the children of Mrs. Noah C. Webster. Her black, down-covered babies, striped with bright orange-red, were crowding the nest by their growth.

Josh watched them from a perch in the low-slung branches of the laurel tree. He noticed especially the network of footprints that the coot had made in the damp sand. The shape of the print caused him to look at the foot that had made it.

"Oh-oh," he said half to himself. "That foot isn't webbed. We'll have to change Mrs. Webster's last name, too."

"What was that?" It was Samuel Surr's familiar voice. "You say you are changing her name again?"

"Well, look at those feet," said Josh. "I don't think *Web*ster is exactly right."

"You are becoming very observant, my friend," Samuel replied. "You are correct. You are looking at a *lobed* foot. Guess you'll have to call her Noah C. Lobster."

The two laughed heartily. The day was off to a good start. The air being cooler than usual, they decided with unspoken agreement to walk rather than to sit in the shade.

"Sir," Josh opened the conversation, "how did you get to know A.B. Simpson if he lived in Louisville and you lived in New York City?"

"Oh, my forgetful old head!" Samuel exclaimed. "Didn't I tell you the rest of the story of that remarkably obedient man?"

Josh shook his head, and Samuel continued. "About halfway through his life, Mr. Simpson and his family moved to New York City."

"Why?" Josh wanted to know.

"Well, Mr. Simpson knew God wanted him to reach people with the good news about Jesus. And he was always careful to do what God wanted of him. Where but in New York City could he have found so many people to preach to? In New York City were thousands of Americans in need of salvation. It was also the gateway to the rest of the world, where great numbers of people lived without knowing about Jesus.

"Do you remember, Josh, who prayed when Mr. Simpson's parents presented him as a baby at their church on Prince Edward Island? It was Dr. John Geddie, a famous missionary to the South Seas. On a monument to him out there you can read these words: 'When he landed, there were no Christians; when he left, there were no heathen.' Mr. Simpson was, in a way, the spiritual son of that great missionary, who many years later reminded Mr. Simpson that he had been dedicated as a baby to be a missionary.

"Also, missionary interest filled the Simpson home as Albert grew up. Albert's father often reminded the family to pray for their missionary friend, John Geddie. When Albert was only nine—not much older than you, Josh, he read the story of John Williams, a missionary who was killed while preaching the gospel in the South Seas.

"You'll remember also, Josh, that from his very first years as a minister in Hamilton, Mr. Simpson's own interest in missions greatly increased his church's interest in missions. The people gave more money to missions than ever before.

"But it was a dream more than anything else that stirred Mr. Simpson's missionary interest. So vivid was the dream that he awoke with a trembling sense of God's power. He remembered every detail of the dream. He had been sitting in a large auditorium with millions of the people all around him. All the Christians in the world were there. He looked toward the platform. It was crowded mostly with Chinese. They said not a word, but they were wringing their hands, and the look on their faces revealed their terrible agony.

"Immediately, Mr. Simpson knew he had seen a vision of the world's people lost without the good news that Jesus could save them. Falling to his knees, he cried out, 'Yes, Lord, I will go!'

"Mr. Simpson was willing to become a missionary himself and carry the message of God to foreign lands. But always something stopped him. His wife, a practical woman with great concern for her children and wanting to see her husband make a name for himself, at first discouraged him. She told him he had received no such vision, and she was not ready to make such a sacrifice. He could go if he wanted to, but she would stay at home and care for the children.

"The mission boards who send out and support missionaries were not very interested in Mr. Simpson. He had too many children and a past history of poor health.

"Still, Mr. Simpson could not forget that clear call he had received to reach the many people of the world. He believed that when Jesus said, 'Go . . . into all the world and preach the gospel,' he had either to go or to be disobedient. Moreover, this was something he should do at once. Had not Jesus also said He would soon return? There was work to do for this soon returning King.

"It was that vision and that dedication that drew Mr. Simpson to New York City. He wanted to be where he could touch all the ends of the earth. So in 1879 he moved to New York to become the minister of the important 13th Street Presbyterian Church.

"The church welcomed the Simpson family with open arms. The people were proud of their church. They were eager to hear how their new preacher would make it an even finer place.

"Mr. Simpson watched his congregation for a while. He was disturbed by some of their ideas. They seemed to be mostly interested in money and social standing and entertainment. Their new pastor knew this attitude would clash with his desire to reach all people, rich and poor, with the gospel. What would he do, for example, with new believers he won as he

preached on the city sidewalks? In his fashion-
able church, only those who had paid to rent a
pew and only those properly dressed were
welcome.

"Where could new believers worship God
and learn His ways if the church would not let
them in? Mr. Simpson was grieved. But, always careful to move only at the Lord's direc-
tion, he thought and prayed for a full week
about what God wanted him to do. At the end
of the week, he was sure he should leave 13th
Street Presbyterian Church.

"It was a Wednesday night when Mr. Simpson announced his resignation. He loved the
people of that church, but he knew God was
calling him to preach to those who did not
know the gospel and not just to some who had
heard it many times. He read from the Bible,
'The Spirit of the Lord is upon me, because he
hath anointed me to preach the gospel to the
poor.'

"My fellow newsmen reported the unex-
pected event. The people of the church were
shocked and filled with grief. They sat with
heads bowed and handkerchiefs to their eyes.
It was a sad night. They loved their minister.

"At Mr. Simpson's home, there was sadness,
too. His resignation from the church meant

that his family, with five children by now, must move out of their lovely house provided for them by the church. They must leave their nice furniture and the carriage which had been theirs to use. No longer would the family have the comfortable salary the church paid their minister.

"Mr. Simpson, concerned for the church he was leaving, urged the members to remain in their church rather than to follow him. But that meant he would have few if any people to support and encourage him. What was worse, many of his friends told him he had made a bad decision. They said he would fail.

"It must have been with a heavy heart that Mr. Simpson and his family left 13th Street Presbyterian Church for their new venture of faith. But Mr. Simpson knew God's will for him, and he must obey. He also knew God would faithfully provide for him and his family."

Samuel became silent. Josh and he continued to walk. Then Samuel began singing:

A hundred thousand souls a day
Are passing one by one away
    In Christless guilt and gloom;
Without one ray of hope or light,

With future dark as endless night,
  They're passing to their doom.

The Master's coming draweth near;
The Son of Man will soon appear;
  His kingdom is at hand.
But ere that glorious day can be,
This gospel of the kingdom we
  Must preach in every land.

"Albert B. Simpson wrote those words, Josh, as well as many other songs that told of his deep desire to do God's will." Samuel was silent as the two reached the place where they would part for the evening.

"Oh, Josh," Samuel exclaimed, "there isn't much left of my old life, but I pray that God will give such vision to young men like you that all the world will soon know that Jesus is Lord. Then Jesus can return in all His glory!"

Samuel paused momentarily again. "Ah, Josh, will that day come quickly? I want to see Jesus!"

CHAPTER
8

He Sees the Outcome of Obeying God

THE SUN WAS SETTING when Josh's family got home from his latest trip to see the doctor. Josh knew he should stay home, but it had been some time since he had seen his friend, Samuel, and he just had to tell him the good news.

With a nod from his parents, he sped across the foot bridge. "Sir! Sir!" he called from the curved center of the bridge as he saw the stooped silhouette of a man under the laurel tree. As Josh approached, a shadowy form turned, stopping the boy dead in his tracks.

"Oh!" Josh said in a startled voice. "I thought you were Sir-ah, Mr. Surr."

"I'm his neighbor," the man began. "And you must be Josh. Samuel thought you might come here tonight. He asked me to meet you. Samuel is sick, Josh—in the nursing pavilion. Would you like me to take you to him?"

"Oh—I—ah—yes, may I see him?" Josh

stammered. Josh said no more as the two started for The Village. His thoughts had already raced ahead to the room where his friend was.

Josh had visited the nursing pavilion before, so the scene was not altogether startling to him. They walked down the corridor and entered Samuel's room.

Josh's eyes went at once to his dear friend. His suntanned face looked healthy enough against the white pillow. Josh walked over to the bed and reached out for Samuel. At the touch of Josh's hand, Samuel stirred. "Josh!" he said with the satisfied deep chuckle the boy knew so well.

"I'm sorry I couldn't come to meet you, Josh," Samuel began. "They have funny rules here about going outside—"

"Sir, are you really sick?" Josh interrupted. "I mean really—are you—what happened? Oh, Sir, are you going to die?" Josh was surprised at his own question. But Samuel approved of the boy's direct honesty. Generations apart, the two were very much alike.

"Yes, Josh, I think I am going to die." Samuel knew Josh could take the truth.

"When?"

"Oh, the *when* doesn't really matter. But

soon, I think. Does that upset you, Josh?" Samuel watched the boy's face as he listened for a response.

"I'll miss you," Josh said, looking his friend in the eye. "I will really miss you."

"Loneliness is something this world knows too much of," Samuel said. "It comes in many forms. Parting is just one of them. But my guess is that you came to tell me you may be leaving me before I leave you. Is that right, Josh?" Samuel hoped to shift the talk to something more positive.

"How did you know?"

"I just knew," the old man said with a momentary upward glance of gratitude. "So you are really well?"

"I'm getting better fast. That's what I came to tell you. But, Sir, you can ask Jesus to make you well, too. I think you're old enough to claim the promises of God yourself." His last sentence was in a slightly mocking tone.

Samuel caught the tease. "I should say I am old enough. And I have asked God about that. He may just surprise me. But as Dr. Simpson said in his last illness, 'We must be willing to allow God to have some of His own secrets . . . we will not know absolutely until we get to heaven.' And I do long to get to heaven,

Josh. Oh, my—" Samuel's voice caught with emotion. Heaven was the only subject he could not find words to talk about.

As best he could, Josh slipped an arm around the old man in the high bed. Samuel reached out and stroked his little friend's head. Regaining his composure, he sang:

Once it was the blessing,
   Now it is the Lord;
Once it was the feeling,
   Now it is His Word;
Once His gift I wanted,
   Now the giver own;
Once I sought for healing,
   Now Himself alone.

"Dr. Simpson's song?" asked Joshua.

"Yes, Dr. Simpson's song, indeed," replied Samuel. "From a child, Dr. Simpson seemed to be set apart for God. He always had a longing to be closer to God. He wanted to know God better than most people know Him.

"Even as a young man, he prayed that he would be a complete Christian and not half-hearted. At one point he feared he would lose touch with the Lord, and the fear kept him awake through the night. Finally at last he realized that he could not hold onto Jesus, but rather Jesus would do the holding. Ah, Josh, what security there is in that! No wonder Dr. Simpson could write:

> *Once 'twas painful trying,*
> *Now 'tis perfect trust;*
> *Once a half salvation,*
> *Now the uttermost!*
> *Once 'twas ceaseless holding,*
> *Now He holds me fast;*
> *Once 'twas constant drifting,*
> *Now my anchor's cast.*

> *All in all forever,*
> *Jesus will I sing;*
> *Everything in Jesus,*
> *And Jesus everything.*

"You will know you are truly obedient to God, Josh, when you can say that Jesus Himself is everything to you. And when you get to be an old man like me you will see that you didn't need anything else. If Jesus Himself is the goal of your young life, Jesus Himself will be the reward of your old life."

Samuel was speaking intensely. His one remaining desire was to see Josh give himself completely to God.

"Josh, I've told you a long story about Dr. A. B. Simpson for just one reason. I told it so you would have an example of how an obedient person lives. Now I need to tell you how the story ends." From some inner source, Samuel seemed to gather extra strength to conclude his long story.

"Near the end of his life, Dr. Simpson remarked that he had lived a lonely life. If you choose to wholly follow the Lord, the path may be rugged and lonely because not all your friends will understand. But remember, Josh, Jesus Himself is enough.

"And in this life also you will have great satisfactions in God's service. Dr. Simpson looked back on the last years of his life and understood how his early dedication to missionary service had been realized. True, he never became a missionary in the same way your parents are missionaries, Josh. But his life was used to reach millions of people with the good news of Jesus.

"After he left 13th Street Presbyterian Church, Dr. Simpson preached to all who would listen. He began one cold afternoon with just a handful of humble, praying Christians meeting in an upstairs room. They were encouraged by a Bible verse: 'Who hath despised the day of small things?' Do you see why I believe God is interested in children, Josh? He doesn't despise small things." Samuel's chuckle brought a beaming smile from Josh.

"From that small beginning grew a mighty church and a variety of activities. As always, Dr. Simpson kept his purpose in life in mind as he began each new thing. Always he asked whether this new activity would bring people to God. If the answer was yes, he endorsed it heartily.

"In addition to founding a church called the Gospel Tabernacle, he and his helpers began a missionary magazine, a publishing company, a bookstore, a city mission, an orphanage, a junior missionary alliance for children, a mission to help girls find honorable work and the house of healing that I told you about.

"As the number of people helping in these activities grew and interest increased, the Christians organized what they called the Christian Alliance. Like their leader, they were dedicated to reaching the world with the gospel. So they also organized the International Missionary Society to send missionaries overseas, to support them while they were there and to pray for them.

"Finally, it seemed wise to combine all these many activities under one organization. They named it The Christian and Missionary Alliance, of which you, Josh, a hundred years later, are a part!"

Such a long recital of the results of Dr. Simpson's life left Samuel almost breathless. And Joshua, wide-eyed, asked, "How could one man do all that?"

"'Not by might, nor by power, but by my Spirit, saith the Lord,'" Samuel quoted softly, his voice weakening.

Josh did not understand, but he hesitated to ask more questions. For a brief time, Samuel closed his eyes, as if to get more strength. Then he continued.

"Dr. Simpson accomplished the work God called him to do by two means: prayer and trust. As a young boy at his mother's knee, you will remember, he learned how to pray to God about everything. He took seriously the Bible verse, 'Pray without ceasing.' And the real secret to his praying was his trust in God. He believed that God could and would meet all his needs 'according to his riches in glory by Christ Jesus.' Knowing that, he could ask God for food when the family had nothing but one box of oatmeal. Or he could pray for the salvation of the 'hundred thousand souls a day' who were dying without knowing God. Nothing was impossible because God is willing to supply every need."

Samuel rested briefly again and then roused to recall one last part of the story.

"Do you know, Josh, what one of my fellow reporters once asked Dr. Simpson?"

"No."

Samuel chuckled. "Reporters sometimes like to ask tricky questions, especially of preachers. But this reporter really wanted an answer to his question. He asked Dr. Simpson if he knew when the Lord was coming back.

"Dr. Simpson said, 'Yes, and I will tell you if you will promise to print just what I say, Scripture reference and all.' The reporter was eager for the answer which the whole world was waiting to hear. Quickly he pulled out his note pad and pen.

"Dr. Simpson said, 'Put this down: "This gospel of the kingdom shall be preached in all the world for a witness unto all nations; and then shall the end come" Matthew 24:14. Have you got the reference?' Dr. Simpson asked. 'Yes, replied the reporter. I have the reference. What more?' 'Nothing more,' Dr. Simpson said.

"Do you see it, Josh?" Samuel asked.

"I see it," Josh replied. "Jesus will come again when all the nations of the world have heard the gospel."

"That's it," said Samuel. "Dr. Simpson knew God. He carefully studied the picture of God's will for his life. And the background of that picture was Jesus' return for His Church. Jesus' return was what urged Dr. Simpson to do what God called him to do."

A gentle breeze wafted a melody from the church chimes through the open window of the nursing pavilion.

> *Oh, how sweet the glorious message*
> *Simple faith may claim;*
> *Yesterday, today, forever,*
> *Jesus is the same.*
> *Still He loves to save the sinful,*
> *Heal the sick and lame,*
> *Cheer the mourner, still the tempest—*
> *Glory to His name!*
>
> *Yesterday, today, forever,*
> *Jesus is the same;*
> *All may change, but Jesus never!*

Glory to His name.

Outside, too, a beautiful sunset painted brilliant colors across the evening sky.

Josh still wore his suit and tie as he sat on the bench he and Sir had occupied so often. He turned the "In Memorial" paper around and around in his hand. He had come to the island in the middle of The Village to remember Samuel T. Surr. The stories they had shared repeated themselves in his mind.

As well as he knew how, Josh renewed his commitment to be like his friend, Sir—and like his friend's friend, Albert Benjamin Simpson—obedient to God. He knew it was the life for him.

As he finally rose to leave, Mrs. Noah C. Lobster was marching her family across the curve of the bridge. He chuckled—like Sir used to chuckle. Then he crossed the bridge, too, on his way to an obedient life.